Bible Stories for . . .

Early Readers

Book 2

I Will Help
The Good Samaritan
Luke 10:25–37

By Lavaun Linde &
Mary Quishenberry
Illustrated by
Joe Maniscalco

1

Jon walks.
Jon walks
on and on.

Men run up to Jon.

The men hit
and rob him.
Jon has bad cuts.
Jon can not walk on.

Rab walks.
Rab walks
on and on.

Rab spots Jon
with his cuts.
"I will not stop
and help him."
Rab walks on.

Lev walks.
Lev walks
on and on.

Lev walks up to Jon
and stops.

"H'mmm.
The man has bad cuts,
but...
I will not help him."
Lev walks on.

Sam sits on Zon.
Zon jogs
on and on.

Sam spots Jon.
"I will stop.
I will help him."

Sam helps Jon.

Sam puts Jon on Zon.
Sam walks with Zon
to an inn.

"Sir, can I get a bed
at the inn
to put Jon on."

"Yes, Sir," the man
at the inn tells Sam.

Sam put Jon on the bed.
"The sun has set,
but I will not nap.
I will help Jon."

"I will fix the cuts
on Jon's ribs
and hips
and lips."

Sam helps Jon
till the sun
is up.
"Jon,
Zon and I
must walk
on."

29

"Sir," Sam tells
the man at the inn,
"help Jon till Jon
is well
and
can
walk on."

Look up John 15:12
and Luke 10:36, 37
to see what God tells
you and me.

Something to Think About

1. What did Sam do all night at the inn?
2. How did Jon feel about Sam?
3. How can I be like Sam at home or on the playground?